Light in our Prisons

The moving account of how one small Christian Diary
transformed the lives of men and women in prison

John Bowmer

DayOnePublications

ISBN 0902548 61 1

Published by Day One Publications
6 Sherman Road, Bromley, Kent BR1 3JH

Front Cover photo: John Millar

Designed by Steve Devane and printed by Clifford Frost Ltd, Wimbledon SW19 2SE

Light in our Prisons

Best beloved of my soul,

I am here alone with thee,

And my prison is a heaven,

Since thou sharest it with me.

Catherine Booth

Introduction

When Prison Chaplain, the Reverend Noel Proctor, wrote to the Lord's Day Observance Society in 1978 asking for a few diaries to distribute among prisoners at Dartmoor, Devon, he little realised that his request would bring about a nation-wide ministry of distributing scripture text diaries to men and women in prison.

The Lord's Day Observance Society responded to Noel Proctor's request by sending 150 diaries to Dartmoor. Just two years later the Society distributed 24,500 diaries to 93 prisons. Half of Britain's prison population received one. By 1995 the number of diaries distributed exceeded 60,000 to 160 prisons and Youth Custody Establishments.

The growth of this outreach to prisoners is a great achievement by any standard, but even more significant is the realisation that hundreds of men and women in prison have found new faith and fresh hope by regular use of the diary. For most prisoners the diary is the only Christian reading matter accepted by them. Many long-term prisoners who would never dream of reading the Bible or a religious book, annually beat a path to the door of the chaplain's office to make sure they don't miss out when the diaries are distributed. Even after release, a number of ex-prisoners write to the Society asking for a copy of the diary and tell of the immense help and comfort it gave them when in prison.

The small, colourful diary, published by Day One Publications and known as the Day One Diary, has a scripture text for every day of the year. The stories retold in this book tell of the amazing way God is blessing and using the diary to bring the light of the Gospel into our prisons. What may seem even more incredible to the reader is the way in which lives have been transformed on no small scale.

Maybe it will take something for some Christians to believe that a prisoner can be a Christian, too. If so, I hope that the stories recounted here will help you to look for the best in the very worst of people. Sometimes we need to remind ourselves that in the gospel narratives Jesus is presented as a man in whose presence the moral failures and outcasts of society felt truly at ease. The sinful Samaritan woman was in need of a Friend and saviour. Jesus reached out in love and compassion to save her; then there is the story of Zachaeus, a fraudulent tax collector, despised by the people, yet singled out in the crowd by Jesus who had a special message of love and forgiveness just for him. In these two examples we can see that Jesus did not accentuate peoples guilt but showed them a far more positive way to a new life. Indeed, throughout his earthly ministry Jesus not only showed the guilty the way but declared himself to be the Way.

There are few words which show us so much about the character and mission of Jesus than when he said, 'I am come not to call the righteousness, but sinners to repentance' (Matt.9:13). When he spoke these words Jesus gave a special message of hope to people who were very aware of their sin and desperately aware of their need of a Saviour. It was sinners who needed Jesus and it was amongst sinners he would move. He simply went where the need was greatest.

Even when he was facing his own death on the cross, he asked the Father to forgive his persecutors. He gave the promise of Paradise to a dying thief and forgiveness to Peter, his failed disciple.It should not be so difficult to accept, therefore, that the living Son of God, who is the same yesterday, today and forever, is able to show the same love and compassion in this age to the shop-lifter, the robber, the murderer, the drug addict, the alcoholic - people in prison for all kinds of crime whose need of him and his gospel is great.

This book, then, should not be seen as a mere catalogue of romantic adventures in the realm of dramatic conversions to Christianity. It is hoped that its pages will provide ample proof that God knows of what material human nature is made, and in spite of knowing our hearts and our failures he commits himself to us, not for what we are, obviously, but for what we can become.

This surely helps us to understand Jesus' dealings with those murderers responsible for putting him on the cross, with the dying thief alongside him, and with the failure of Peter. It also explains, perfectly, how people in prison can find new faith and hope through the use of a diary because God is still able in this day and age to deal with peoples failures and sins through his written word wherever it is read, even inside prison.

The following are just a selection of people whose divine - human encounters proved to be the beginning of a healing relationship in which God, in love, reached out and met the emotional and spiritual needs of people in prison. Prisons became sanctuaries, darkness was turned to light, 'the grace that is sufficient' transformed lives. The day of miracles is not passed.

AGE: 24 RELIGION: Church of England. LOCATION: Styal.
Janet was sent to prison just two days before Christmas day, having been convicted of shop lifting. This young mother of two tiny children was described in her initial reports as being an 'aggressive inmate'. Then she received, rather reluctantly, the gift of a Day One diary and her whole life was changed.

AGE: 21 RELIGION: Methodist. LOCATION: Ashwell.
David came from a good family background, was well educated and for-tunate to be in a good job. Long before he was twenty-one he reckoned he was a man. He was quickly acquiring a taste for alcohol until he found himself in prison, on remand, on a rape charge brought by his for-mer girl friend. His direction in life was completely turned around when he read the scripture texts in the Day One diary given to him by the prison chaplain.

AGE: 56 RELIGION: Methodist. LOCATION: Garth.
Leslie was serving a five-year sentence, after admitting to trying to kill his wife, when he had a life-changing experience. The scripture texts in his diary reminded him of the unlimited love of God for the repentant 'prodigal son'. Now out of prison, Leslie claims that he is a living wit-ness to the Bible truth: 'All things work together for good to them that love God.'

AGE: 17 RELIGION: Pentecostal. LOCATION: Rochester.
Gary, at the age of seventeen was serving his third custodial sentence. This time, eighteen months for robbery with violence. Two years earlier he rebelled against the Christian upbringing which his parents had attempted to 'force' upon him. Lacking courage to speak to the prison chaplain about his spiritual condition, Gary wrote to the Lord's Day Observance Society whose address was on the cover of his Day One

diary. Resources were harnessed to help Gary see that there are more important values to life than the monetary ones which had ultimately led to his downfall.

AGE: 55 RELIGION: Church of Scotland. LOCATION: Glasgow.
James was a Company Director serving three years for fraud. He found his Christian background made it harder to come to terms with his prison sentence but his life 'inside' took a turn for the better when the text in his Day One diary brought him to the place of questioning, not to the validity of Christianity but about himself and his relationship with God. James is now more acutely aware of the mistakes he has made in the past but he will tell you that the biggest mistake of all was when he left the Christian path and went his own way.

AGE: 39 RELIGION: Pentecostal. LOCATION: Leeds.
George found an unfriendly and hostile world waiting for him when he was released after serving a six year prison sentence for burglary and theft and he was totally unprepared for it. He just couldn't cope with the loneliness. He thought the only solution was to end his life, which he was about to do when his thoughts were arrested by a text given on the very page of the diary on which he intended to write his final farewell. 'The words seemed to come alive' says George, 'and I am alive today rejoicing in God's goodness in my life'.

AGE: 23 RELIGION: Not known. LOCATION: London.
Not every story has a happy ending and perhaps Norman's story will serve as a timely reminder to some of the sheer frailty of humanity. Norman's trouble was that he was hopelessly addicted to hard drugs. He had high hopes for the future but most of all he had a deep longing to be freed from the addiction that held him in its grip. The Lord's Day Observance Society also had high hopes for Norman every time we sent him a Day One diary. But then he vanished to appear no more until we heard of his tragic death.

AGE: 19 RELIGION: Roman Catholic. LOCATION: Maidstone.
Martin's mother, at the end of her tether, only wanted to shock her wayward son and knock some sense into him when she literally dragged him into the police station. Unfortunately, in surrendering her son to a crim-

inal justice system she surrendered him to a system that was not so much to reform his behaviour as to make it considerably worse. Fortunately the decline was halted when Martin began to make daily use of his diary.

AGE: 56 RELIGION: Church of England. LOCATION: Isle of Wight.
John considered himself an atheist and considered the Bible, which he had never read, rubbish, until he started to give thought to the scripture texts printed in his Day One diary. Never did anyone pray a more desperate prayer than John as he knelt down in his prison cell and prayed the only prayer he knew, taught him by his mother long ago. There at his bedside, with a child's simple trust, devoid of faith as he was, George knew that his prayer was being heard.

AGE: 60 RELIGION: Church of England. LOCATION: York.
Alfie, who became a Christian in the early days of serving a life sentence, has discovered a source of strength from reading the daily text in his diary and he is always ready to share his discovery with other prisoners and prison officers alike.

AGE: 25 RELIGION: Church of England. LOCATION: Holloway.
Enid had a privileged upbringing and was a sophisticated young lady who enjoyed life in the fast lane. One day, whilst serving a prison sentence for drug related offences, she turned to her Day One diary and what she read revealed to her the emptiness of her life. She knew she had to make a choice. Either surrender her life to God or continue her past life-style with its inevitable consequences. She decided to give God a chance.

All involved in this work count it a priviledge to be able "to proclaim freedom for the prisoners"(Luke 4.19)

Gratitude is surely the greatest response we can give to God for the wonderful way in which he has used the Day One Diary to b ring his saving grace to the lives of these people when in prison.

The Lord's Day Observance Society also acknowledge with gratitude the generosity of many churches and individuals who have made the distribution of the diary possible. Your gifts can never be measured in monetary terms, their true value will one day be counted in eternity.

People at crisis point

Prisons are full of people. There are bad people, sad people, old people, young people, fit people, ill people, professional people, ordinary people, the guilty and sometimes the innocent. All kinds of people yet all have one thing in common. They are people at crisis point. People needing to discover the goodness of God and to be reassured of their own self-worth.

Any reader unfamiliar with the prison system can never fully understand what it means to be 'sent to prison'. There are few who would deny that imprisonment is very largely an act of punishment and of retribution; that it needs to be harsh, potentially soul-destroying and at times brutal. The majority would probably argue that it is as it should be, or that, if anything, the trend these days is towards too much leniency and comfort.

Certainly it is true that in the last few years there has been a noticeable improvement in the atmosphere of our prisons. The original basic elements of the well ordered Victorian gaol - food, shelter, clothing, exercise(of a sort), religious services, and medical treatment are still in place but there are now work opportunities, access to books, education facilities, and provision for social life and recreation. Some of Britain's penal institutions are bright and airy places. A small but growing number of prisons are newly built, and the very newest have finally made the ultimate concession to the twentieth century by providing either individual lavatories in cells or allowing night access to communal facilities. For the prisoners fortunate enough to be placed in these modern prisons the humiliating ritual of slopping out is a thing of the past.

But this is only one view. Anybody listening to accounts of imprisonment from ex-prisoners, particularly from those who have experienced prison life in our severely overcrowded and outdated prisons, and they are still very much in the majority, will find it hard to reconcile what they hear with some of the official claims about prison conditions. Ex-prisoners consistently emphasise the harshness, the depersonalisation and the overbearing aimlessness of life in prison. Only a small minority find going to prison a respite, a haven, a place providing comfort and warmth compared with the park benches and cardboard boxes of a hostile outside world. For most, even the hardened and highly experienced, being in prison is a time of stress and fear.

Most of us do not even think about what it means to be in prison. We have a picture of a Prison Officer in a uniform with a peak cap, jangling keys, a rule book, a disciplinary system, small cells and an institutional routine which fits reasonably well with those we send to prison. We may have some vague notion that the prisoner's family suffer from the separation and that the State ensures that any financial hardship is be kept to the minimum. Most of us do not have the wildest notion that a person in prison ceases to exist except as an automation at the mercy of an arbitrary system.

On being sent to prison, often long before conviction and sentence, the prisoner is no longer thought of as a person. Instead the prisoner becomes a number. The outside world carries on as before, but the man or woman in prison has no part of it, nor influence over it, a greatly reduced awareness of it, and very little contact with it. Told when to use the lavatory, when to collect food, when to exercise, when to go to bed, when to rise, the prisoner has no independence of action, little freedom of choice, less a person than a thing. This loss of individuality means a loss of dignity and once an individual's dignity is lost the personality is all but destroyed.

The burden is made even more intolerable because it is necessarily accompanied by a loss of liberty. Nothing, nothing at all, can compensate a person for the loss of his or her most precious possession - freedom. Most evenings a free person can relieve stress by relaxing at home with his or her family, enjoy intimate moments special to husbands and wives in love, or socialise with friends at a club or community centre. Being deprived of the opportunity to weep or reveal deep feelings is, for some, the hardest aspect of imprisonment. The prisoner has no friends inside prison, only casual acquaintances in whom it is impossible to confide. A person in prison has to survive alone; physically cut off from society, separated by high walls, with barbed wire on top to foil climbers, with entry from outsiders governed by strict rules and regulations. Only those who have experienced the severe deprivation that results from a complete loss of liberty can really know what being in prison is like.

To help you have some idea of what it means to be in prison close your eyes and imagine for a moment finding yourself obliged to stay in a hotel so overbooked that you have to share your room with two complete strangers. The room itself is so cramped that there is little space for your clothes or personal possessions, and if you want to move around the other occupants must first lie on their beds. Worse, the hotel management insists that guests remain in their rooms for all but an hour a day and must take their meals there. As a result, the atmosphere rapidly becomes unbearable, especially since neither you nor your room mates have been able to take a bath for some days. But not only is there no access to the bath, you cannot go to the lavatory either, and you and your companions are faced with the prospect of relying for the foreseeable future upon chamber pots thoughtfully provided by the management. Imagine having to face this kind of degrading experience not just for seven days, but for several months and possibly years!

The conditions under which prisoners on remand are held appear to be considerably worse than those of convicted prisoners. Remand prisoners are locked in their cells nearly all day and have few recreational activities. This seems to be particularly unfair since something like 40% of all remand prisoners are eventually judged to be innocent or are given a non-custodial sentence. Yet the rate of increase in remand prisoners continues to outstrip all other groups of prisoners. Protecting the law-abiding public from these alleged offenders, it is argued, is a greater priority. Thus the prison population has continued to grow, reaching levels which now, according to prison officers, threaten a major catastrophe.

The mission statement of the prison service states: *"Her Majesty's Prison Service serves the public by keeping in custody those committed by the courts. Our duty is to look after them with humanity and to help them lead law abiding and useful lives in custody and after release."* The reform of prisoners, however, provokes concern. Anyone who has examined the penal institutions cannot escape the conclusion that prisons by their very nature do not as a rule turn men and women prisoners into law-abiding citizens. Only the naive will believe that those imprisoned are prevented from evil.

As institutions where offenders are sent to be punished, prisons are very much the product of the Industrial Revolution. Built in or close to large expanding areas of the urban population, prisons like Pentonville(1820), Leeds(1840) and Leicester(1850) were intended as ever present reminders to those who broke the social contract that punishment involved incarceration behind their awesome towering walls. Of course there were prisons before the Industrial Revolution, but they were used mainly for those on remand and for debtors who were normally held under more flexible conditions. Relatively few offenders were sentenced to prison and as such, they were more likely to be transported or to suffer bodily punishments, such as whipping, branding or the ultimate penalty – hanging.

During the course of the Industrial Revolution this emphasis began to change. There was a shift away from punishments directed at the body to punishment aimed at the mind. This reflected a feeling, an optimism almost, that under the right conditions men's minds might be completely recast; that offenders could be resocialised to lead a good and useful life. This great enterprise was entrusted to new model prisons using highly developed systems or technologies of control based on surveillance, classification and instruction.

Still, this so called modern form of prison reform is, in the main, proving to be futile. Can any amount of reform ever produce a prison system capable of transforming offenders, call it rehabilitation or whatever? The simple truth is that our modern prison system is about punishment and deterrence and nothing else. If the prisoner, after being punished, is only deterred by fear from further imprisonment, he or she is not reformed. Reformation is more than giving up certain habits and steering ones life to avoid clashing with the law. It implies a change of character and a change of heart and only the Grace of God, through Jesus, can bring that about.

Sceptics may question the ethics of encouraging people who, in prosperous and happy times want nothing to do with God. Yet the history of the Christian church has shown that it is people at crisis point who are most able to hear and respond to the good news of the gospel. This is why people in prison are surely not only in enormous need of the gospel, but also of great openness to it. Maybe this explains why the Day One diary distributed to prisons by the Lord's Day Observance Society is so popular among prisoners. It is as Augustine once said, 'You have made us for yourself, and our hearts are restless till they rest in you'.

From crisis to Christ

J anet had been a happy wife and mother, but now bitterness, frustration and despair were part of her life. One day, without warning, her husband walked out of the house and did not return. Left penniless and having inherited massive debts accrued without her knowledge, Janet found there was no shortage of people ready to lend her money. Her first concern was for her two young children, aged three and five. They had to be fed and clothes were getting more expensive as they grew older. The youngest child suffered from epilepsy and attacks were distressingly frequent. Weighed down with worry, she became easy victim of the loan sharks who charged extortionate rates of interest on the smallest amount of money borrowed. Very quickly her weekly outgoings far exceeded her social security benefits and her debts spiralled out of control.

Terrified she would lose her home and maybe her children being separated from her and placed in the care of the local authority, Janet resorted to crime. Shop lifting, she thought, was her only chance of survival and of keeping the family together. At first she took only a little at a time, and only occasionally as need determined. Socks, underwear, tinned food. But then the number of incidents escalated and she became more daring, stealing increasingly expensive articles, ranging from coats and shoes through to household items.

Janet was surprised at how easy it was to shop lift and get away with it, but she was even more taken aback at the manner in which she had so easily become hooked on this form of criminal activity. She had always maintained high standards of morality, decency and honesty in her life. But she justified her crimes because they were done for the sake of the children. And life had been so unfair to her that she felt she owed nothing to anyone.

It was at night, however, when the children were asleep and she sat alone in the living room of their small, sparsely furnished terraced house that fear of the consequences inevitably got to her. The strong feelings of loneliness and rejection, ever present since her husband had walked out on her several months earlier, became insignificant in comparison to the fear she felt. At night she lay awake worrying she would one day be caught. Inevitably it was not long before she was.

Janet was arrested one grey November morning after being caught stealing toys 'because she wanted to give the children a happy Christmas'. Just two days before Christmas Day she appeared before a judge in the Crown Court where she admitted the offence. Desirous of wiping the slate clean she asked for twenty other offences to be taken into consideration. The probation officer told her to expect a probation order or at worst a suspended prison sentence. She was totally unprepared for the severity of the eighteen-months prison sentence, not suspended, which the Judge imposed.

Separated from her children, stripped of all human dignity and respect, overcome with anguish, despair and feeling of injustice against her and the children, Janet's prison cell became a living hell. The prison chaplain visited her on Christmas Day. He had the onerous task of trying to offer cheer to a disconsolate young mother, whose fierce maternal instinct had turned her into a very bitter aggressive inmate. He felt it prudent to make a hasty retreat, but before doing so he gave her a copy of the Day One diary– a gift which she totally ignored.

Not many days later Janet received a letter. It was from her husband who she had not heard of or from since the day he walked out on her. He was seeking a divorce. He wanted to marry someone else. Janet was absolutely distraught.

She still loved him, in spite of what he had done and she had always held secret hopes that one day he would return to sort things out. She longed for them to be together again and share the happiness which they once knew. Now, the letter she held in her trembling hands destroyed all her hopes that one day the love she held for the only man she had ever loved since her father died when she was just six years old, would be reciprocated once again.

The prison authorities became concerned about the emotional and psychological condition of this woman who often considered that suicide was the only escape from the cold realities of the prison cell. In her mind her life had come to an end. She lived, but yet she was dead. Her actions became mechanical. She ate, not knowing what was on her plate. She rarely spoke but sobbed continuously, her body racked with fits of shaking, her shoulders never still of the spasms that gripped her. But always she thought of her children. What were they doing? Were they safe? Was Philip behaving himself? How was he getting on at school? Was Angela eating her breakfast without gobbling? How was her epilepsy? In restless sleep she called for her husband, even though the divorce was proceeding. Why didn't he love her anymore?

Because of their concern the prison authorities asked the chaplain to try and talk to Janet. Even he was alarmed to find her in such an emotionally disturbed state. But instead of the anger and bitterness so evident when he first met her, he found a woman overcome with self-pity. 'Please help me,' she pleaded, 'I can't stand any more. Help me, help me' the burdened woman mumbled between sobs.

Unopened and unused on the table close by lay the diary left there on Christmas Day. Picking up the diary the chaplain sensitively asked Janet what the important days were in her life. When were the children's birthdays? Did she know the date of her release? Turning the pages of the diary he encouraged her to talk about those things which were important to her and of her children who still loved her and needed her. He talked to her about brighter times to come. 'Now isn't always,' he said. Then he drew her attention to the text for her own birthday which said, 'all things are become new'. The chaplain asked if he could pray with her and while she was being prayed with her tears flowed heavily down her face. An experience which Janet later recalled 'was my first real encounter with God and the beginning of God's working in my life'.

Up until this time Janet had never felt the need to consider whether or not she believed God existed. The only time she had come into contact with religion was when her father died and the vicar called to make arrangements for the funeral service and to read a prayer from a book. Even then she was banished to the room next door, for at six years of age she was considered to be too young to share in any family grief. She was not allowed to attend the funeral itself. Instead, she was taken care of by one of the neighbours.

She can never remember a time when her father was not poorly. His illness, whatever it was, prevented him from going to work like her friends' fathers did, consequently they were always poor. She remembers vividly her mother telling the folk who came to the house to offer their condolences. What a relief it was, now that he was gone. Not many weeks later Janet was introduced to a man who, she was told, was to be her new Dad. It was a bewildering moment coming so soon after the loss of a Dad who she loved dearly - and she has never forgotten it.

From then on Janet's childhood was not the happiest of times. Her mother and step-father were always quarrelling which sometimes led to physical violence, especially when her step-father was drunk. To make matters worse for Janet, all of the folks in the close-knit community seemed to know, and the family became social outcasts; certainly nobody of Janet's age wanted to be her friend. She wanted to run away but had nowhere to run to. 'I wanted to reach out and live a normal life in a happy home, like other children,' said Janet. 'When I get married,' she thought to herself, 'I'm not going to let this happen to my family. I'm going to make a proper home for my kids.'

'God, if you are there, why are you doing this to me? Why have you taken my children away from me? Why? Why? Why? screamed Janet after the chaplain had gone . 'I was angry at God, I shouted at him. I even told him to go to hell, said Janet, when recounting her first conversation with God. 'I was in a really bad way. All my ambitions to make a good home for my husband and children were gone for good. I couldn't stand it any longer. I just had to shout at God because if he was in control of things, like the chaplain said he was, then he was to blame.'

In the quietness of the late evening Janet felt a strange 'presence' with her in her prison room. 'It was weird,' recalls Janet, 'as if God was beginning to answer me back, but not shouting at me like I had shouted at him. He was just telling me that he loved me and wanted to forgive me. He was telling me how much he knew about me, about my thoughts, my distress, my heartache'. Janet felt compelled to look again at the scripture text in the diary, the one which the chaplain had talked about.

Turning to the date of her birthday she read again and again the scripture text, 'all things are become new'. 'Through these words in the diary Jesus was telling me that I could be a new person right there and then. It was the most indescribable thing that was happening to me.' Janet spoke to God again. This time she didn't need to shout because she knew without any doubt that he was the 'presence' with her. 'God, come and help me, because I need help. I really need help.' Says Janet, 'From the time I uttered that prayer I've never been alone since.'

Meanwhile, by a remarkable coincidence, some forty miles away from the prison, Janet's two children, Philip and Angela, were also being introduced to Jesus, the friend of little children. It should be remembered that the bottom had fallen out of their world, too. They had not been prepared for the separation from their mother at a time when they were already emotionally vulnerable after the mysterious absence of their father from their young lives. They had reacted badly to the loss of Daddy, now they needed a very special kind of foster parents, folk who would provide more than just a home, with food, and hand-outs.

'Aunt' Mary and 'Uncle' John fitted the bill admirably. They gave the quality of loving care which made the children feel wanted, and more besides. Because Mary and John were Christians and active church members they had a spiritual dimension on life which they were able to pass on to the children. Bedtime prayers played an important part in keeping Mummy close to them and helped resolve many of their fears. Their regular attendance at Sunday-school gave a sense of belonging. But unknown to Aunt Mary and Uncle John, they were also building the early foundations to a Christian home which was to emerge following their return to Mummy.

The rest of Janet's story is a continuing one of a gradual deepening of her relationship with Jesus. In the weeks which followed, the prison chaplain, in patient instruction concerning the Christian life, taught her about the nature of sin within all of us and told her about God's remedy for our sin through Jesus Christ. Step by step, getting to know him better, overcoming many difficulties and testing experiences on the way, Janet indeed became a new person, just as the scripture text in the diary said she could become. She is now happily reunited with her children and serving the Lord as leader of a mother and toddlers group at an Evangelical Church in West Yorkshire. She is also married to Alan, a committed Christian. Together they are making the kind of loving, caring home which Janet once dreamed of in her childhood for themselves and their three children, yes, there are now three.

'When I told God to go to hell, I didn't think he would come into my living hell and rescue me from it, but he did. When I was experiencing the greatest crises of my life he brought me to Christ who forgave me for all the things I had done which were wrong.'

To any person troubled by personal circumstances, whether emotional, social or spiritual, Janet recommends her Lord and Saviour, Jesus Christ, confident that he is the answer to every need .

Honest before God

David awoke with a start and embarked upon the agonising process of surfacing from the effects of alcohol. He looked around for the familiar furnishings of the bed-sit room which was home, the usual litter of empty bottles, the heaps of discarded clothing across the floor, the pile of dirty dishes filling the kitchen sink. Were the voices that he could hear those of his companions? If so, what were they doing outside?

Soon his muddled brain told him he was not where he thought he was. There was something unfamiliar about his surroundings. The room was bare, his bed felt unusually hard. But it was the bars on the window which attracted his attention. He looked in dismay as it slowly dawned on him that he was in a police cell and the voices outside were those of police officers.

How did he get here? He could only vaguely recall having a conversation with police officers the night before but he had no idea what it was about. 'Don't panic,' he told himself, 'there's nothing to worry about.' Once sober he would be charged with a drunk and disorderly offence and released on bail to appear before a magistrates court on some future date. He would plead guilty and receive a fine. His friends had been through the system many times before and lived to tell the tale, 'no sweat', he thought.

David strove for reason when, later that same day, he stood in the local court room, flanked on either side by two police officers, accused of the attempted rape of his former girl friend. Because he could remember very little about the night before, he was unable to give a satisfactory account of his activities but he was 'quite certain', he told the magistrates, that he was innocent of the charge. He tried to explain how the sheltered home into which he had been born and his Christian upbringing had impressed upon him that there were some things which decent people did not do, and raping women was one of them. Not surprisingly, perhaps, there appeared to be a distinct look of disbelief on the faces of the magistrates when they ordered him to be remanded in custody to await a full trial.

It is true that David's parents are good, kind people, who considered it important that their son attended Sunday-school, a place to which he regularly set off but at which he seldom arrived. He showed the same lack of enthusiasm for day school, 'My teachers agreed that I was thick in the head,' David recalls. On leaving school my standard of academic work was laughable.' Even so, David successfully applied for a place on a computer programming course at a local Technical College.

At college he found himself surrounded by educationally qualified people. The sensation of inferiority was a rude awakening. But the moment of self-revelation was also one of high resolve. From that moment David began to push himself beyond his limits in his determination to make the grade and his efforts paid off when he secured a good job in the city. His parents were proud of him. The future seemed to be promising and secure.

Things began to go wrong when one Sunday, with nothing to do, he went to a pub used by some of his former college students. David was not used to spending time in a pub but he felt it was time he renewed old friendships. He quickly became hooked on the atmosphere and unknown to him, he also became hooked on alcohol. 'I couldn't keep away. After I drank my first pint I had to have another then another,' David recalls. He became apathetic towards his work and lost interest in his home and family life. 'I felt more at home in the pub, the people I met there were my kind of people.'

David's change in life style quickly alienated him from that of his parents. The secure, happy, family environment in which he had lovingly been brought up no longer appealed to him. He eventually moved out and rented a one room flat, situated just a few doors away from his favourite pub. It was too convenient to invite friends round for drinking sessions after the pub closed at night. Soon the word about this meeting place spread and the number of David's friends increased. All types came, usually bringing a bottle or can with them, and the flat became a venue for many a wild party.

It was at this point that David came in contact with drugs. He had never seen them before, never mind use them, but his curiosity was aroused. He tried one, then another kind, then another. He started by smoking "pot" and taking pills. Then he took harder drugs, the real mind twisters. He began to miss days and even weeks from work. Helplessly, his work colleagues watched his promising career go down the drain. Painfully, his parents watched his life speed down the road to self-destruction.

David was no stranger to confrontations with people who tried to help him. His parents, work colleagues, folk from the church all tried in vain to counsel him. Each time he became acutely aware of his own shame and of the distress he was causing his family. Each time he promised to leave drink and drugs alone. Each time he failed to keep his promise. But this time, as David faced the judgment of the court he knew that he was in serious trouble. Rape was a most serious offence. If proved guilty he would be given a very long prison sentence.

He still held strong feelings of affection for the girl who was now accusing him but David knew that under normal circumstances he would never, never, force himself upon her. There was no pseudo-bravado as he protested his innocence by declaring he was not that sort of person. But in his heart David knew he had made a total mess of life and that often his behaviour was far from normal.

'What a mess,' cried David as he tried to settle down for another night in a prison cell, one of many which he knew he would have to endure. He was still feeling numb after being remanded in custody just hours before. Two or three days later a Methodist Minister, who was also a part-time prison chaplain sought out David. 'I was amazed to find that he already knew a great deal about me and my family,' David recalls. 'He asked me if I wanted to overcome my problem with the drink. I said that I did. He asked me if I had ever prayed about it, and I could honestly say that I had. Many times, usually when I was in trouble I had prayed, and even though I usually finished my prayers in a stream of blasphemy, deep down I was seeking. The Minister asked if he could pray with me, and he did. He asked God to come into my life and help me in my troubles. Before he left the minister asked if I would like to have a diary. I said, yes.'

David spent six months on remand which gave him plenty of time in solitude to reflect upon his life. He could not get the minister's prayer out of his mind. Was it really possible for God to come into his life and help him in his troubles, even inside this prison? he wondered. 'One night I was looking at the diary which the minister gave me. Whether as a result of reading the texts or by the direct intervention of God. I don't know, but quite involuntarily I fell on my knees and in deep humility began praying to a God. I was quite unable to control my actions or my emotions. I just knelt on the floor with great tears streaming down my face. It was like a dream, crying, just crying and yet feeling so light-hearted I could have jumped for joy!'

On the first day of his trial David brought a most honest prayer from the depths of his heart to the Lord. 'O God!' he prayed, 'You know if I am innocent or if I am guilty. If I am guilty forgive me for it and through your forgiveness give me your peace. If I am to be sent to prison give me strength to face the dark days ahead. That's why I am really praying. I cannot face the future without you. If I am innocent and I am set free, help me to follow you for the rest of my days so that I will never be in this situation again.' Once again tears streamed down his face as he poured out his heart to God. But when he rose from his knees David knew that the Lord was with him and that his future, whatever it was meant to be, was in God's hands.

Even so, it was with a strange mixture of confusion, shame and an indescribable calm that David stood before the judge and jury in the Crown Court. His conscience told him he had not lived a blameless life; far from it. He was selfish and irresponsible, wild and lazy. He was ready to tell the truth, that he remembered very little of the night of the alleged offence. Yes, he knew the alleged victim very well. They had been going out together regularly some months previously. No, they had not had a sexual relationship during that time. Yes, he was still fond of her. No, he had never had sexual intercourse with any other girl. And so the evidence proceeded.

The trial lasted for two days during which three of David's companions who were with him on the night of the alleged offence gave evidence in his defence. The probation officers report highlighted David's home background and the Christian influences in his life, and his regret at going his own way and the remorse shown for the pain caused to so many people. The report referred to his rediscovery of God during his time on remand. It took less than two hours for the jury to find him not guilty of the charge. David was acquitted.

At the first opportunity he went along to the Methodist Church where he used to attend Sunday-school. 'For the first time that I could remember I went willingly,' said David. 'I was amazed at the warm welcome I received. The minister took a special interest in me and guided me through those early days of my new life in Christ. I discovered that members of the congregation were interested in my future, not my past. Their support and encouragement was unbelievable.'

David has met Gillian at Church and a loving relationship is emerging which both partners feel will lead to marriage and the establishment of a caring Christian home. David says that the diary given to him will remain a treasured 'keepsake', not as a reminder of his nightmare experience of prison, but of the night when the minister's prayer was truly answered and God came into his life.

Spreading the word

Distressed beyond measure, Leslie found it impossible to settle down to life behind prison bars. As a middle aged, intelligent, hard working family man of previous high integrity, he was totally unprepared to cope with his five year sentence. To Leslie the circumstances which brought him to this situation were like an unbelievable dream. He had, however, admitted to attempting to kill his wife in mitigating circumstances. But through this one, irrational act, everything of importance to him, his home, his children, his work and the wife who he still loved, all he had lived for, were lost forever. He was a broken man without a future.

In his distress, Leslie became conscious of an inward desire for God to begin to work in his life but he felt too ashamed to take his desire seriously or do anything about it. In his earlier years he had been a member of the Methodist Church in his home city of Sheffield but he admits to never having entered into a personal relationship with Jesus Christ during this time. Never-the-less he maintained a loose connection with the church right up to being sent to prison. Unknown to Leslie, there were members of that church praying for him. People who believed that the ever present, all powerful Grace of God, can be found at work in seemingly unlikely places. Even inside jail.

Shortly after being transferred from Armley prison, Leeds, to Her Majesty's Prison at Garth, near Preston, Leslie was handed a Day One diary by the prison chaplain and he unexpectedly discovered the daily scripture text to be a source of strength to him. Those inward longings to put things right with God began to surface again as Leslie became an avid student of the scripture verses. Leslie found its pocket size handy for carrying the diary around prison into places where the Bible could not be realistically taken.

The diary became a ready reference as he sought to come to terms with his situation. The more of the scripture quotations he read the more he became aware of God's love for him as a person in spite of his wrong doing, and as he became more and more enveloped in God's love, so his desire to return that love grew inside his heart.

'The day came,' says Leslie, 'when I dared to ask the Lord to forgive me for my wrong doing and to help me to live a Christ like life.' His prayer for forgiveness changed to a prayer that was a promise to God. 'I will follow you. I will devote my life to telling other people about you,' he promised. And in that moment, without another human being to counsel him, Leslie became a committed Christian. 'God has not only forgiven me but He has also given me joy in my soul,' Leslie declares.

Leslie became a regular worshipper in the prison chapel and an enthusiastic member of the weekly Bible study group. Sometimes he was able to fulfil his promise to tell others about God's love by bringing other imates with him to the study group. And that in itself was quite an achievement, because few prisoners incline to any form of religious practice in a positive way.

No longer was Leslie's idea of a Christian someone who went to church on a Sunday. 'I realised for the first time that being a Christian meant having a personal relationship with Jesus Christ,' he says. 'I enjoyed talking to the Lord as to a personal friend. My knowledge of the Bible was shameful yet I knew that the indescribable joy in my soul was the work of the Holy Spirit and I was growing in the faith. My hunger for more of God knew no bounds.'

When Leslie was released from prison he was apprehensive about how he would be received into a church and how he could keep his promise made to God. Against his own wishes Leslie was released to Boxtree Cottage, Bradford, a home for ex-offenders run by the Langley House Trust, a national Christian charity working for the care and support of ex-offenders and their families. But things moved quickly and amazingly well for Leslie after this. The warden of Boxtree Cottage took him along to a nearby Mission hall where he was warmly received into the Christian fellowship. He was given a variety of manual jobs to do within the Mission and later doors of opportunity for further service among the large ethnic community opened for him.

Leslie knows that he is where God wants him to be. He believes in work and prayer, and does a good deal of both. Above all else he wants to lead people to Christ. Not many may be as desperate as he was when he knelt down in his prison cell. Even so, Leslie firmly believes that everybody needs Christ. To a world with so many problems, personal and social, Leslie offers his Saviour, confident that he can put things right. And to the task of leading at least some to him he is fully given up.

The responsibility of leading others to Christ, indeed the privilege of doing so, is felt by many prisoners who experience the same 'joy in the soul' as Leslie. Alfie, who became a Christian in the early days of serving a life sentence accepted the responsibility of sharing his new found faith from the moment of his conversion. He looks forward to receiving his diary each year. He puts his order in to the chaplain as early as July. He already has five diaries covering his time in prison and he says that they are among his most valued possessions. Alfie has discovered a source of encouragement and strength from reading the daily text, and he is always ready to share his discovery with other prisoners. Consequently, among the dullness of prison despair, Alfie often has a shine to him.

On one occasion Alfie was praying quietly, his voice scarcely audible in his cell. A fellow prisoner who walked in was curious. 'Are you talking to me?' he asked. 'No,' said Alfie, 'I am speaking to God.' The prisoner walked hurriedly out of the cell and sought the nearest prison officer. 'That bloke in there is a bit of a nut. He says he is speaking to God.' Even the officer didn't understand so Alfie quickly took his Day One diary and began to explain at length the meaning of the text for the day which said, 'Call upon me and I will answer you.' The next day the prison officer quietly asked Alfie where he could obtain a diary like his.

Peter, a prisoner freed from drug dependency and who has known the Lord for some fourteen months now openly declares his dependence on Jesus. Writing in the Preston prison prayer and praise newsletter he comments: 'Isn't it a pure joy to awaken each day to God's unfailing love; to reach out for the mighty hand of God to help and sustain us throughout the day ...However, I would like to take this opportunity to share with you what Jesus has come to mean to many of us in our day to day sentence. Prison, being a closed community, does present many problems for us when we confess our faith.

'Sometimes we are ridiculed, sometimes we do face contempt and scorn, but when compared with the priceless gift we have received through Christ Jesus, this seems a very meagre price to pay. Often we feel very privileged to suffer for what we believe. There is also another side to this. Many inmates do realise and witness men being changed before their very eyes. When they see that this is a genuine decision that has been made, many will express more than a passing interest and even come to respect those who follow Jesus.'

Peter continues, 'In an often depressing place, it is wonderful to see the faces of those who have come to know Jesus. We do sometimes have bad times, but today's bad times are much better than yesterday's good times when we did not know the Lord.'

Leslie, Alfie and Peter might all say like the Apostle Paul, "Having therefore obtained help of God, I continue unto this day, witnessing both to small and great alike.... that Christ would proclaim light to his own people and to the Gentiles" (Acts. 26.22)

A better thing

Gary, at the age of seventeen, was serving his third custodial sentence. This time, eighteen months Youth Custody for robbery with violence. His prospects did not look very promising. Two years earlier he had rebelled against the Christian upbringing which his parents had tried to enforce upon him. Early teenage scepticism had crystallised into outright agnosticism. He felt that the God spoken about in Church only catered for the sentimentality of older people or added spice to the fairy tales told to children.

Gary himself felt he had no need of God. Why should he? He was already of the opinion that if anyone was to prosper in this life they needed money. Money meant influence and power. 'No Divine person up there or wherever could give me that,' said Gary. 'I gave my parents a pretty rough time before eventually leaving home to seek my fortune on the streets of London.'

Like many others before and after him, Gary soon found that the streets were not paved with gold and before long he was caught up in the not unfamiliar London scene of drugs and male prostitution. Although Gary was anything but at ease with his situation he still believed that money would bring him the elusive secret to life's happiness. How he obtained the money and at whose expense did not enter into the plan to achieve his goal. One unsavoury act led to another until Gary became well and truly hooked on crime.

He became a familiar figure in the magistrates courts, and in detention centres before being sent to Rochester Youth Custody Centre where his values on life were about to change.

'It all started when the Chaplain came through the block on one of his morning visits and he asked me if there was anything he could do for me. As usual I said "Nothing" but on this occasion the warm expression on his face and his friendly manner reminded me of the people back home, my parents and the folk at the church which they attended. There was something about this man which seemed to tell me that, like them, he was someone who cared. Although I was always making fun of him and his religion, he kept coming back and asking if there was anything he could do for me.

Back in my cell I thought about how I had reacted towards the chaplain earlier in the day. I did not know what it was at the time but I saw something in him that I was lacking. Yet in the days that followed I could not raise the courage to speak to him. Perhaps I was afraid of how the other inmates would react if they saw me sidling up to the chaplain. So whenever he came and asked the same question on whether there was anything he could do for me, I gave the same answer, "Nothing".

At the time I was using a little diary which the chaplain had given me at Christmas to tick off the days to my release. Not that I had much to look forward to after my release. I was still too proud to return home and I knew it would be hard to find a job because of my record. I opened the diary and there I read the text for the day, "God provided some better thing". At that moment I began to realise there must be something worth striving for other than money, although I wasn't sure what it was. I knew that the chaplain would be the one person to help me but I still lacked the courage to tell him on one of his visits that there was something he could help me with.

Then I noticed on the diary cover the name and address of the Lord's Day Observance Society, the organisation which had supplied the diary, so I wrote to them seeking help. By return of post I received a Bible, some books and a very helpful letter telling me that the chaplain would be coming to see me. He came the same day and we had a long talk.

One day he brought my parents to see me - the first time we had met face to face in nearly two years.' In the seclusion of the chaplain's office, tears flowed freely while understanding and forgiveness sealed the reconciliation. Gary promised his parents that he would be a better son, one in whom they will one day be proud. 'It was a very emotional reunion,' Gary recalls, 'but one for which I am thankful today.'

The good news is that the promise made has been kept. Gary has been living with his parents for nearly two years now, and he has a steady job working in the office of a private coach hire company. He is engaged to be married. Gary says, 'I wouldn't say that I am a committed Christian in the sense of being an active member of a Church, although I do go along with my parents on special occasions. However I do believe in

A better thing

God and I now know that the Christian way of life which my parents tried to teach me is the only right way. I shall always be grateful for Christian people who cared enough to show me that essential values of life are spiritual and not material. It is as the text in the diary said it would be, "God has provided a better thing".

Then there is the amazing 'better thing' wrought in the life of Enid as a direct result of using her Day One diary. Enid was a sophisticated young woman, daughter of a wealthy industrialist and a socialite mother. Enid lived life to the full, the kind of life that was possible only to one in a privileged position. She attended Church with her family on special occasions but this was only a charade. For Enid, God was a threatening figure, although she readily acknowledged his existence. Sometimes she allowed herself to thank God for her privileged position. But in reality she had turned her back on him and the formality of religion long before she was sent to prison.

Enid tells her story. 'I was on drugs and I was wild, absolutely wild, enjoying life in the fast lane with my jet set friends. Never did I think that I would one day be sent to prison as a result of my life-style. This was my life and I wanted to live for kicks without anybody telling me that I couldn't. With hindsight I admit that I lived only for the present with no thought for the harsh reality of the future.'

For Enid that harsh reality was prison where she was sent for nine months after being convicted of a drug related offence. Given the diary at the conclusion of the prison carol service, Enid immediately began to use the gift to highlight significant dates - visiting days, parole eligibility and date of release being the most important of all. Usually a prisoner's release date is what occupies the mind more than anything else but the vagaries of the parole system means that there can never be certainty when that date will be. Enid says that for her, the diary was her one link with the outside world and a key to unlock the devastating affects which imprisonment had on her mind.

One day Enid discovered that the diary held the secret of another kind of release on the mind which, since her conviction and sentence had been racked with shame and tortured with guilt. As she turned over the pages of the little diary she read with increasing interest the scripture verses. 'And what I read,' says Enid, ' revealed to me the emptiness of my life.'

'I began to realise that for years I had been stifling my own nagging doubts about the real meaning of life, and love and death and beyond. I was more intent on putting on a good show of "being with it" in front of my friends.' Enid felt that she could not face the task of trying to put things straight within herself, probably because she was afraid of the outcome and too afraid of the results of her own neglect. In truth, she didn't really know how to begin.Nevertheless she knew she had to do something with her life, but what?

She knew it was one of two choices. To follow the God whose words were speaking to her heart from the pages of the diary, or continue on her release from prison with her high society style of living with its inevitable consequences. Enid reflected on the many painful experiences of recent weeks - her arrest, humiliation, shame - and decided there must be lessons to be learned somewhere. Enid decided that God's way must be the better way and whilst she does not claim to have had any instant conversion experience there and then,('I neither offered repentance or sought forgiveness at the time,' says Enid) the decision was the beginning of a new life which was to change her whole purpose for living.

Now released from prison, Enid firmly believes that the greatest sin is to be conscious of no sin. 'Once I acknowledged my sin before God and claimed his forgiveness I was overwhelmed by his love and with a desire to show his love to others.' Enid worships regularly in her local parish church and spends as much time as she can talking from her own experience to young people on the dangers of drugs.

Praying for courage

When one considers that each of our prisons contains hundreds of prisoners of whom a proportion, almost by definition, will be cunning, unscrupulous, and not necessarily attentive to their own best long-term interests, it will be obvious that prison is the hardest place on earth to declare by word and by deed that you are a Christian. It takes courage to stand up and speak out for Jesus. It is not surprising, therefore, that not all Christians in prison make an open declaration of their faith.

Prison can be a cruel and vicious place depending where the prisoner stands in the rigid hierarchy of prison values. Within the scale anyone seen 'to be a good boy or girl' is considered to be in pursuit of dubious ends and therefore treated with the utmost suspicion. Many prisoners, because they are cynical and bitter, see anyone trying to live a Christian life and to openly witness to their faith, as an inmate with ulterior motives. Claiming to be a Christian is considered to be no more than a grovelling exercise, and a way of gaining merit points in the parole stakes. Therefore any Christian inside prison can expect to be on the receiving end of considerable persecution. Even minor irritations such as having their food oversalted, nothing but cold water left for the weekly bath, being handed the most worn and torn shirt from the stores, all come dangerously close to bringing the most zealous Christian to the point of total defeat.

James is six feet plus of lively Christianity and is representative of many other Christians currently serving a prison sentence who are subject to such persecution. For the past eighteen months he has been incarcerated in Barlinnie Prison which has a reputation of being one of the most brutal and inhuman penal establishments. Nestling beside the busy M8, some three miles from Glasgow, Barlinnie is an awesome looking building. Its five main residential halls hold some 900 prisoners in conditions which make some of England's Victorian prisons seem almost Hilton-like. Here the atmosphere is tense, doors bang all day, officers scream and shout. The prison clothing, red and white striped shirt and woollen baggy trousers made from army-type blanket material, do nothing to instill any degree of self-respect. James is serving a three year sentence after being convicted of fraud. Before this his life was expansive. He travelled a great deal, he lived well enough. As a businessman he made good money. He was a company director, with talent and entrepreneurial skills. His Christian upbringing equipped him well to serve for twenty years as an elder in the Church of Scotland. However, when James decided to expand his interests from the Plant Hire Business which he directed into establishing a leisure park in the Scottish Highlands, his commitment to the church took second place and eventually he drifted away altogether.

James admits that his obsession to be a successful businessman above all else, caused a barrier between God and himself which he later found difficult to break down. After he had made the 'stupid mistake' leading to his arrest, James felt the need to attend a place of worship whilst waiting for his trial. For several weeks he attended The Salvation Army in Perth where his heart was once again warmed to the good news of the gospel and to the fellowship of believers.

James found it all the more difficult to settle down to prison life. He is a proud, family man. A man of intelligence who likes to be useful. In prison he was acutely conscious of his downfall, his pride had been seriously damaged, his intelligence starved, and his skills impaired. It can truly be said that his life fitted the dictionary definition of the word 'prison': one deprived of freedom of action or expression.

What does a man from a Christian background do when his life has fallen apart and he is stricken with remorse and regret? He seeks out God and cries to him for help. At least this is what James did. Shortly after being given a Day One diary James felt that God was speaking to him through the texts contained in the diary. He was challenged by the verse 'Where your treasure is, there will your heart be also.' Looking at the text, emotion turned to questioning, but not to the truth of Christianity. His questioning concerned himself. He knew that he had got his priorities wrong. God had taken a lesser place in his life than he demanded. That night James' prayer of desperation changed to a prayer that was a promise to God. 'I will follow Your way. You will have first place in my life,' he promised.

Praying for courage

James quotes Psalm 40 as his favourite portion of scripture because, he says, the words best sum up his testimony: 'I waited patiently for the Lord; he turned to me and heard my cry. He lifted me out of the slimy pit, out of the mud and mire; he set my feet on a rock and gave me a firm place to stand. He put a new song in my mouth, a hymn of praise to our God. Blessed is the man who makes the Lord his trust ...'

Even so, living the Christian life in prison is far from easy for James in spite of his restored relationship with God. It would appear to the onlooker that the spiritual life of the prisoner is well catered for in most prisons. In Barlinnie the Anglican full-time chaplain is well supported by a team of part-time chaplains from a cross-section of the denominations. The chaplaincy office has an 'open door' policy to all prisoners, whatever their race or religion may be.

James has the utmost respect for the chaplain and his team and is thankful for their ministry but he is fearful of seeking counsel and help because of the ridicule he is likely to face from his fellow prisoners. James will not usually be found in chapel on Sunday morning, either. Although the chapel is quite full he feels that this reflects more a desire on the part of the men to spend the maximum amount of time out of the cells than to commune with their God. He claims that a number of men attend chapel in order to get a good parole. Once they receive a favourable parole date they cease to attend. James finds this largely indifferent attitude of the prisoners makes worship, for him, a depressing experience.

But James has turned his prison into a place of prayer, his bleak cell into a chapel and a sanctuary. He finds great comfort from reading his Bible and continues to find help and guidance from the daily texts in his diary. He has also forged links, through correspondence, with the church in Uganda, which he knows well. The knowledge that Christians there are upholding him in prayer is a source of strength to him. But James, and all other prisoners striving to live the Christian life in the hostile environment of prison need the prayers of us all.

For some prisoners the future is uncertain. John is one who, because of the unhappy domestic relationships with his family, is not sure what the future holds but is appreciative of the prayers being made on his behalf. After years of indifference to religion and after once telling the prison chaplain that the Bible was rubbish, God has given him a gladness he has never known before.

His opinion of the Bible, which incidentally he had never owned or read, changed after he accepted the gift of the Day One diary. Within six months of accepting the diary from the chaplain he returned to tell the chaplain that he had found Christ. His frequent use of the diary meant he could not escape from reading the daily verses and from the moment the scripture texts arrested his attention God commenced a work in his heart. The verses helped John to see that, even for him, there was an open way to God.

John was already acutely aware of the hurt he had brought to his wife and two teenage children as well as to the victims of his life of crime. Whilst in prison he took the lid off himself and was ashamed with what he found. Now, as sin weighed heavily upon him until he ached with the burden, he saw in the diary words which spoke of the intensity of the love of God. Punishment for his crimes he knew he deserved, but the forgiveness of Christ, revealed to him in the scripture, brought repentance to his heart. His desire to pray was compelling. Never did anyone pray a more desperate prayer than John as he knelt down in his prison cell and prayed the only prayer he knew, taught him by his mother years ago, and it began:

> *Gentle Jesus, meek and mild,*
> *Look upon a little child,*
> *Pity my simplicity,*
> *Suffer me to come to Thee*

There at his bedside, with a child's simple trust, devoid of faith as he was, he knew that his prayer was heard.

Pray for James and John and other men and women in prison who are seeking and striving to live the Christian life.

God never gives up

Martin was literally cast up on the doorstep of the local police station. His tall, well proportioned and muscular body, which made him look far older than his sixteen years, towered over his comparatively small mother as they stood side by side in the reception area, while his mother recounted his misdeeds, pronouncing him beyond hope. 'So far as I am concerned you can take him out and shoot him,' she said finally - and she meant it.

Martin's interest in things athletic in which he excelled, and the fact that he had a black belt for Judo, made him, at a very early age, a valuable member of the gang of youths which terrorised the community in which he lived. Night after night Martin would be on the streets with his friends looking for a fight, and he would not return home until he had played his part in beating some unfortunate victim 'senseless'. His peer group lived in fear of him.

His antipathy toward school, where he paid little attention to work or studies, disrupted the class and bullied pupils, led to the school management refusing to have him anymore. With an inevitability on which a betting man would gamble his last shirt, Martin was drawn into membership of an infamous group known as the ICF Gang, which went around the country causing riots at football matches. Knives, coshes, spiked knuckledusters, studded boots all became essential tools of his pastime.

At home Martin took everything and contributed nothing, but worry, fear and heartache to his gentle mother who tried hard to provide a loving, comfortable environment for her only child. His father had left home when Martin was just four years old and had had two wives since and children by them both. His good intention of keeping in touch and providing for his estranged wife and son had long since been forgotten. For years Martin's only contact with his father was when he saw him with his latest partner going home from the pub late at night.

Martin's mother, at the end of her tether, meant only to shock her son and knock some sense into him when, with all the strength she could muster, emotionally and physically, she dragged him along to the police station and 'spilled the beans' as it were. The police couldn't believe their luck. They had been trying to collect evidence against Martin and his friends which would be admissible in court for some considerable time and here it was being given to them on a plate. Martin was taken into custody and placed in the temporary care of the local authority pending his court appearance.

Sadly for Martin, this turned out to be the beginning of a spiralling downward path towards a life of crime involving burglary, theft and robbery. In the home where he was placed he met another youth with a similar affinity for violence, except his was of a sexual nature. Within a few hours of meeting, Martin assisted his new friend in a sexual assault on a younger boy in the home before absconding together. On the run from the police, Martin and his friend needed a safe hiding place, money and food, and they used every criminal instinct within them to obtain these, usually by mugging an unsuspecting person on the street, or when this failed, breaking into a house or business premises and helping themselves to anything useful.

Martin was caught just one week after absconding from the local authority home. Because of the serious nature of the new charges against him he was held in the security of a remand centre pending his trial. It came as no surprise to Martin when he was eventually sent to a detention centre for three months. At the centre Martin's reputation quickly became known and the tougher inmates soon began to jostle each other to be associated with him, like courtiers wanting to be next to the King on his throne. But this grouping was tinged with a certain awe. Martin sensed that most were afraid of him and his cunning nature quickly surfaced to take advantage of his status. Even with the restraints imposed within a prison establishment Martin found plenty of opportunities to bully and exploit other inmates, particularly the weaker ones.

Martin's violent and criminal lifestyle continued for a further two years during which time he spent another three months at a detention centre. It was whilst serving his third custodial sentence, this time for a term of twelve months, that Martin came to his senses. A person in prison is usually a prisoner to his or her thoughts and feelings. For several weeks Martin had been recording his thoughts for each day in the diary given to him on his admission by the chaplain. To make the excercise more interesting Martin summed up his thoughts in just one sentence. Each day he read the scripture text but initially he was not conscious of the daily verse making any impression on him.

One Saturday, Martin was reading over what he had written in his diary and at the same time taking note of the texts for each day. Gradually, Martin came to a sense of self-realisation that his life had been a total waste. 'I was wicked. The knowledge of what I had done and what I was capable of had always been lurking deep inside me but I didn't care. Every man for himself was my philosophy.'

Now he was asking himself the question, 'What am I doing with my life?' Although he had had a tough childhood he was making no excuses. It would be easy to pass the blame onto his deserting father but his mother had more than compensated for the loss of any fatherly love and protection. Martin admitted to himself that he, and he alone, was to blame for his situation.

Martin resolved to discard the criminal codes which had ruled his lifestyle so far. But where could he go for help? Surrounded by young criminals whose lives were just as mixed up as his was, and with his life being controlled by prison officers who Martin felt would only respond to his cry for help with derisively comments, he felt totally alienated from any source of support. 'If ever I needed my mother, it was at that hour,' Martin recalls. Then he remembered the words of the chaplain when he was handed the diary. 'It is my job to help you,' he had said.

Martin asked to see the chaplain who was very kind and understanding, not at all judgmental. 'I was struck by the sympathy he showed towards me. He seemed to genuinely want to help me. I accepted his invitation to attend the service in the chapel on the following Sunday. Not that I was becoming suffused with religious fervour, it was just that I wanted to show the chaplain how grateful I was for befriending me. The service itself was sheer bedlam. Inmates heckled their way through the readings, cheered loudly if the chaplain said something popular and booed when he said something they didn't like. After the service, I returned to my cell feeling frustrated and angry that my inmates should treat the chaplain in such a manner. I wanted to give them a good hiding. 'Here we go again,' I thought, 'will I ever get away from my violent streak?'

'I had never owned a Bible. In fact the only time I can recall handling one was when taking the oath in court, but when the chaplain gave me a copy I began to read it with enthusiasm - secretly, of course - I did not want the other inmates to see what I was reading.

'I can't say that I became a Christian when inside,' says Martin. Victory over my violent nature and bad temper was not easily won. Even after my discharge I had my rocky periods.' But one of the things Martin learned is that God never gives up on a person. Now, three years later, Martin is six foot of living Christianity. He is by no means overpowering but he is a compelling witness to the power of God to transform lives.

'I have entrusted the worst and the best of myself to God and he is blessing my life in so many ways in return,' says Martin. And he adds to his testimony 'I firmly believe that from the point of receiving the Day One diary God had a plan for my life. All the frustrations that I was suffering, all my mixed up emotions, even the evil which was ruining my life seemed to subside when I began to use the scripture text diary.

'I don't blame my mother for washing her hands of me and surrendering me to a criminal justice system which was destined not so much to reform my behaviour, as to make it considerably worse. The lesson has to be learned that casting young offenders into institutions does not cure the escalating crime rate - it causes it. Only God in His mercy can make bad people good.'

Coping in a hostile world

It is difficult for anyone who has not been in prison to know what happens to the mind of a prisoner after a short time. The truth is that even after a short time inside a prisoner becomes institution-alised, to the extent that when the release date draws near, the prospect of such a change in surroundings becomes alarming rather than exciting.

The first day out is undoubtedly, for the majority of ex-prisoners, a critical occasion. To be a prisoner one day and a responsible citizen the next inflicts too great a strain on men and women whose capacity to cope with stress is already suspect. Partly because of the time spent in isolation from society, there are a whole range of problems and fears confronting them: the noise and density of traffic, *and* the task of physical survival in busy streets; coping again with money, and with prices which may have changed out of all recognition; dealing with shops and shop assistants; coming to terms with the renewed presence of people of the opposite sex; the semi-paranoid feeling that everybody is looking at them and recognising their background. But in addition to this, there is the even more difficult task of surviving by one's own efforts. For so long the prisoner has had no decisions to make, no responsibilities to carry, no problems to cope with. They feel they are in a hostile world. Those who are on their own continue to feel the stigma of imprisonment for longer than those with a social circle to which they can turn.

One of the greatest hurdles a discharged prisoner faces when he leaves prison is getting a job. The first question any employer will ask is where have you been working for the last few years. Being honest at this point carries with it the likelihood that you will remain unemployed. From the very first day, therefore, the discharged prisoner has to start rebuilding his or her life on a foundation of lies in order to survive. The debt to society may be paid, but the receipts are never written.

Implicit recognition of the damage that is done to a prisoner's capacity to survive in the outside world is made by the Home Office's development pre-release facilities to ease an inmate back into the community. Geared to the needs of prisoners serving sentences of four years or more, its purpose is to help inmates through the critical period of transition from a closed institution to the open society. In essence, a prisoner who is selected for the scheme is allowed to take work outside the prison for about the last six months of the sentence.

Although George had been on the Home Office pre-release scheme it failed to equip him for the kind of world he faced following his release - a lonely, hostile world. George came out of prison feeling he did not have a friend in the world. His family were all dead. Former friends and acquaintances turned away when they saw him in the street. Nobody, it seemed, wanted to associate with a man who had just come out of prison. George's freedom turned into a different kind of personal prison. 'I had the feeling I would never be happy again; my only thought was to end my life.'

Despairingly George reached into his pocket for a pen and something to write on. All he could find was the Day One diary given to him in prison. Intending to write a suicidal message for the authorities who would have to deal with his affairs, George stared at the open page, blank but for some small print next to the date. Before he could put pen to paper his thoughts were arrested by what the small print said, 'We have peace with God through Christ.' He read the words over and over again and gradually he became aware that the peace he was reading about was overwhelming his shaking body. Was he imagining in his depressed state that God, whom he had refused to have anything to do with for years - since he was a boy - was speaking to him in his hour of need?

In those far away days he had gone regularly to church in the little town where he was born, for his mother was a church-loving woman and insisted that her boy attend too. But it didn't mean anything to George and when he was about sixteen and his mother could hold him no longer he left home and went his own way. His mother prayed that he would not go too far astray, but after George had left home and adopted a way of life in which he was so sadly confirmed, it seemed that her prayers had no chance of being answered.

George was an habitual thief. He began his criminal career by stealing from the pockets and handbags of his work colleagues. When he was found out he lost his job. But he failed to learn his lesson for he was dismissed from his next job also after being caught stealing from his employer. His landlady became his next victim. And so the pattern continued until George hit 'the big time', breaking into houses, usually those belonging to the wealthy, where his haul often ran into thousands of pounds. Two prison sentences failed to halt his addiction to crime; as soon as he was released he returned to living on the receipts of his many criminal activities.

Then came his third and longest prison sentence - seven years - from which he had just been released. Now the subconscious belief and influences of his Godly mother began to stir and surface as he continued to focus on the text in his diary. 'You can end your life here, but what about eternity? You will not find the peace you are seeking there unless you first find it here and now,' were the thoughts that went through his mind.

Those thoughts held George back from carrying out his suicide mission. Instead he made his way to a nearby church where he was welcomed into the fellowship and shown the way to God and his salvation. A new person was born. 'My heart was relieved of its heavy burden', says George. 'I have found peace with God'.

George wrote to the Lord's day Observance Society on the autumn of 1993, asking for four Diaries for 1994. One was for his own use, the other three were for 'friends', friends which he once thought he would never have again.

Sadly, not every story has such a happy ending. In the summer of 1994 the National Press reported the tragic death of Norman who was befriended by the Lord's Day Observance Society after he received the gift of a Day One Diary. Like George, he failed to discover his true worth in the sight of God. When his death by suicide was reported by the tabloid press, it treated with cynicism the fact that the only item found in his pocket was the Day One Diary with its scripture texts.

We had become very fond of Norman and it was an enormous blow to all of us involved in the prison ministry when we heard of his death. We are thankful to God for the 'success' stories arising from our work, but Norman's tragic death reminds us that society still has its failures. For this reason, we have devoted a chapter to Norman's story, and included in it our own thoughts on such a wasted life.

'If only....' are words which have passed our lips many times since Norman's death. If only Norman had realised that there was a way out of his situation, and not a new way at that. If only Norman had understood that Jesus came to lift the downtrodden, restore the lost, heal the broken spirited, give strength to the weak. If only Norman had realised that even in his failures God still actually believed in him. If only Norman had confided in people who also care because God cares. If only Norman had met and talked with some of the people whose stories of restored lives are told in this book. If only.......

Lament for Norman

Lament for Norman, for Norman is dead! We all feel very sad about this for from the first moment when he made himself known to the Lord's Day Observance Society, nearly six years ago now, we have been drawn to him, not that first appearances would attract anyone to him. His skeleton like figure is covered in skin sores, his eyes large in comparison and heavily matted. Norman used to write to the society every year from which ever prison he was in at the time asking for his own 'very special' diary.

Norman's trouble was that he was a drug addict. Hopelessly addicted to hard drugs. He was given just two years to live by a prison doctor and every few weeks, following his release on parole in the summer of 1992, he made his way to a clinic for a prescription and check up. Yet he was intelligent, having a number of A levels and with a keen perceptive mind which was recognisable even when in a drugged state. He came from a good Scottish family and told us often that his parents were concerned about him.

He first experienced drugs as a school boy then he turned to them in adulthood as a means of escape from the problems of life. For a time on his trips he found release only to come back to a harder reality afterwards. From soft drugs he turned to hard ones so by the time he reached his twenty-first birthday he was a hopeless addict. Lots of people tried to help him. He spent brief periods in three different drug rehabilitation units. He was found several jobs with sympathetic people but his utter unreliability led to failure upon failure. When all else failed prison became inevitable.

Every year Norman's letter would tell us of his hopes for the future but most of all of his deep longing to be freed from the curse of drugs that held him in its grip. He became a very special friend to us all. Following his release on parole, Norman, having rejected the offer of a communal home for ex- offenders, occupied a caravan on the outskirts of Newcastle. He shared his home with a Labrador dog to which he became devoted. We had high hopes. But then he vanished to appear no more until we heard of his death by suicide.

Immediately we felt a sense of real sorrow. We thought of Norman's desire to be free of his craving and to live a useful sort of life. We thought of his wasted gifts and talents, of his parents who had such high hopes for their son. We thought of his gentle, loving nature so evident in the way in which he cared for his dog, often sacrificing his own food to make sure Butch had enough to eat.

Oh, Norman, what a tragedy, what a waste. We know there are too few answers to problems such as yours but taking the hard route out as you did is not one of them. We had hoped the diary we gave you at Christmas 1993 would have pointed you in the direction of the One who could have helped you face your problems with confidence. Still, you must have found some comfort in its pages, for we are told that when your lifeless body was discovered the only possession on you was your diary, which when opened was seen to have one of the daily texts heavily underlined. The text read, 'Have mercy upon me, O God according to Thy loving kindness.' We do not ask it as an easy glib solution to restoring our shattered hopes but we do pray that your prayer will have been answered at the end.

Letters of appreciation

The measure of which the diaries are appreciated is evident in the following comments received from both chaplains and prisoners.

"The men tell me how much they appreciate not only having a means of jotting down reminders of family anniversaries but also they are encouraged by being brought face to face with extracts from the Scriptures. Several times during the year I have been asked about a particular passage and some have followed up with a request for a copy of the whole Bible."
Chaplain, HM Prison, Coldingley.

"We continue to use the Diary texts as the basis of our Bible class meetings. Recently four lads made an open profession of Jesus as Saviour and Lord."
Chaplain, HM Young Offenders Institution, Dumfries.

"The diaries are much appreciated by the inmates. Recently one of them told me his release date was February 19th and the text was, 'You must be born again'. He said he was going to pray for it to happen."
Chaplain, HM Young Offenders Institution, Stoke Heath.

"The men come into my office with well thumbed, crumpled diaries. I see them sticking out of back pockets and shirt pockets. The men do not want to leave them where they can be stolen. They are truly valued."
Chaplain, HM Prison, Wetherby.

"The diaries are a firm favourite. One Nigerian lady who was here and had a diary last year, but who has since returned to Nigeria, has

written to me asking for a 1994 diary. It is as if, as another prisoner once said to me, 'the Word of the Lord is unstoppable."
Chaplain, HM Prison, Styal.

"My apologies for asking for more diaries. I wouldn't ask if they were not needed or used so effectively here. Because this is a Young Offenders Institution many of the lads are experiencing prison for the first time. The diaries give them a daily focus as they mark off the days of their sentence. The lads use them daily to record their thoughts and impressions. They often mention to me one of the verses that they have been reading on a particular day and what it has meant to them. The diaries are an important part of my ministry."
Chaplain, HM Prison, Stoke Heath.

"Your Diary gives a Bible text for each day. You will be thrilled, as I am for I have just heard the testimony of a young man in the Block. Without anything else to do, he had picked up the Bible left in the segregation block cell to look up the context of the text given in the diary for that day. Suddenly the word made sense - he is reborn! The light shines in his eyes. He will shortly leave this Category B prison for a Category C prison where he will soon qualify for home leave. He has been praying for time to learn more and to see his family.
You cannot tell Kevin that prayers are not answered! Your Diary first prompted him – he is just one of many."
Chaplain, HM Prison, Garth.

"I should like to reassure you that the diaries are very much appreciated by our inmates here. One lad remarked that he loved looking up the short text each day and then seeing the context in which it came in the scriptures. Great!"
Chaplain, HM Prison, Stocken.

"The men were asking for the diary well before their arrival and it was a great joy to receive your parcel just before Christmas so that we were able to meet the demand from the men. In past times men have often mentioned how a particular scripture verse for the day meant something to them and I know that these are appreciated and that the Word of God is sown as a seed through the daily text. One can only

give thanks to God for all the generosity of His people who have made such gifts possible to be sent to all our prisons. It is indeed a very tangible symbol of the Christmas message that God so loved the world that He gave His only begotten Son, and in your giving we do receive something of God's love."
Chaplain, HM Prison, Leyhill.

"The diary acts as a journal for prayer....it can become a map of emotion, and a tool which helps the reader pass the days with a written companion."
Chaplain, HM Prison, Askam Grange.

"Thank you on behalf of the lads who are fortunate to get a diary. It is very important to have something of your own in prison - even more so when that small possession has the ability to comfort and inspire."
Chaplain, HM Youth Custody Centre, The Mount.

"A new inmate was feeling anxious about a family situation outside. His cell-mate felt that the text for the day in the diary would help him. As a consequence of this he came to see me to talk things through. He asked for a diary but unfortunately we had run out (they are in big demand here). He went away with a Bible and a Christian book. On Sunday he went to our Church Service and from that came into the Bible Study Group. God can use these diaries in such ways....opening doors for us to bring the Gospel of our Lord Jesus Christ to bear."
Chaplain, HM Prison, Bedford.

"I feel I ought to write again to say how much your diaries are appreciated by both staff and inmates. The 1,000 you sent me have almost gone, and there are still men asking for them. Both staff and inmates have said how impressed and helped they have been by the verses of Scripture which are read and digested each day. The requests for diaries begin in October, so it shows how much they are appreciated."
Chaplain, HM Prison, Strangeways.

"On behalf of all our inmates, I thank you for all the diaries you so kindly sent to us. Because of your generosity, I was able to give every

man one; and they were well received. Comments were forthcoming such as 'I like to follow the texts and readings', and, 'Oh good! It starts on the proper day'. Apart from the usefulness of the diary, they are a great source of inspiration and witness. They are also a wonderful way of reaching many who may otherwise show no interest in Godly matters."
Chaplain, HM Prison, Huntington.

"As you know the diaries are much sought after by all inmates. I always make a point of drawing their attention to the daily readings, but it was one of the inmates who drew my attention to the change you have made by introducing 'What to use when...' and 'Where to find.....' This will certainly be widely used. One lad who became a Christian this year has been facing a great deal of pressure from other prisoners. I've been thrilled that each time I meet him, he is able to quote the verse for the day, and share its relevance for him, as well as ways in which he has been able to share with others."
Chaplain, HM Youth Offenders Institution, Dumfries.

"The texts in the diary are not only read but frequently used to introduce a friendly discussion. As you know all too well, in every penal establishment there are a wide range of individuals from the 'hard men' to the 'easy-led' and immature. As your kindness permits us to circulate the diaries so the Spirit speaks through the printed word and who can tell what changes follow."
Chaplain, HM prison, Perth.

"The diaries are a very helpful point of contact for me and a means of getting to know individual prisoners. Although a diary might not seem very significant to us, for the prisoner it is a real gift."
Chaplain, HMYO, Onley.

Letters from prisoners:
Sometimes prisoners themselves write letters of appreciation to the Lord's Day Observance Society and express ways in which they have been helped and blessed by the use of the diary. Often the letters reveal

searching minds and seeking hearts after the things of God. Here are some examples:

"Your diary has been such a wonderful help to me this year I was wondering if I could impose on you and request that you send me another for next year."

Prisoner, HM Prison, Maidstone.

"I would like to take this opportunity to thank you all for supplying the Day One Diary. It is not only very useful for keeping track of day to day events, but also helpful in providing a daily reflection for those who like me, are spiritually out of sorts."

Prisoner, HM Prison, Wormwood Scrubs.

"Thank you for sending the diary. I was feeling very depressed and lonely until I read the quotations. They were just what I needed as I have started to read the Bible which helps me a lot.

I just want to say keep up the good work you are doing. The lads here really appreciate the diaries and use them to record their EDR (earliest date of release), LDR (latest date of release), PED (parole eligibility date), also birthdays and visiting days. A lot find the Bible quotations helpful in times of crisis. I hope you can send more diaries next year. Thank you."

Prisoner, HM Prison, Grendon.

Christh is the answer

We may continue to send men and women to prison but if we want to reform the offender we must recognise that the underlying cause of much that makes prisons necessary is spiritual in nature and that the Christian message of God's love as seen in Jesus is the answer.

I am convinced that the only hope for this sad world of ours lies not in more prisons or even in a closer study of the statute book, but rather in a reappraisal of Bible teaching; not in external control, but internal regeneration. The people whose stories have been told in this book are testimony to this.

There is one more thing to say. If Christ can become so real and so satisfying to the people in this book who were brought to him through the influence of the Day One diary, why shouldn't you, wherever you are, have a similar thrilling experience? If you are concerned about your spiritual condition and you are not sure what to do about it, the Lord's Day Observance Society will be pleased to point you in the right direction. Write to:

LDOS, 6 Sherman Road, Bromley, Kent, BR1 JH.

Epilogue

A certain man had two sons. "And the younger of them said to *his* father, 'Father, give me the portion of goods that falls to *me.*' So he divided to them *his* livelihood.

"And not many days after, the younger son gathered all together, journeyed to a far country, and there wasted his possessions with prodigal living.

"But when he had spent all, there arose a severe famine in that land, and he began to be in want.

"Then he went and joined himself to a citizen of that country, and he sent him into his fields to feed swine.

"And he would gladly have filled his stomach with the pods that the swine ate, and no one gave him *anything*.

"But when he came to himself, he said, 'How many of my father's hired servants have bread enough and to spare, and I perish with hunger!

"I will arise and go to my father, and will say to him "Father, I have sinned against heaven and before you, and I am no longer worthy to be called your son. Make me like one of your hired servants."

"And he arose and came to his father. But when he was still a great way off, his father saw him and had compassion, and ran and fell on his neck and kissed him.

"And the son said to him, "Father, I have sinned against heaven and in your sight, and am no longer worthy to be called your son.'

"But the father said to his servants, 'Bring out the best robe and put *it* on him, and put a ring on his hand and sandals on *his* feet. And bring the fatted calf here and kill *it,* and let us eat and be merry; for this my son was dead and is alive again; he was lost and is found'. And they began to be merry.

"Now his elder son was in the field. And as he came and drew near to the house, he heard music and dancing. So he called one of the servants and asked what these things meant.

"And he said to him,'Your brother has come, and because he has received him safe and sound, your father has killed the fatted calf.'

"But he was angry and would not go in. Therefore his father came out and pleaded with him.

"So he answered and said to *his* father, 'Lo, these many years I have been serving you; I never transgressed your commandment at any time; and yet you never gave me a young goat, that I might make merry with my friends. But as soon as this son of yours came, who has devoured your livelihood with prostitutes, you killed the fatted calf for him.'

"And he said to him, 'Son, you are always with me, and all that I have is yours. It was right that we should make merry and be glad, for your brother was dead and is alive again, and was lost and is found."

Luke 15:12–32